Damaged Little Creatures

ೞ

Leona Sevick

FUTURECYCLE PRESS

www.futurecycle.org

Published by FutureCycle Press
Lexington, Kentucky, USA

ISBN 978-1-938853-67-8

For my children, Elijah and Adah Jane

Contents

White

Instead, I spotted our mother in a tiny
chair in the back row, her blue-black head
shining unnaturally. She was dressed in

clothes she'd laid out carefully in her
mind the day before, when her hands
were moving along spools of every color,

bright rainbow of threads flying through
air as loud as a train. It cost her half a day's
piece-work to see her boy and girl out-read them all.

Her own English, bent and twisted still, even
after all those years, carried whiffs of garlic and
fish sauce. We hoped she would be silent.

At home, where every night we waited for
the rice to steam, her soft chatter lulled us to sleep.

They say that Alfred Hitchcock was afraid of lawmen

Holding the dog by one brown paw,
you looked like you were shaking hands—
old friends you never were.
The dog, new dead, held her head against
your thigh. She seemed at gentle play,
except for the angle of her lolling tongue
that looked like graying salmon. I watched you
stroke her ear between your finger and your thumb,
and I recalled a story from your working life,
when you'd picked up that drunk on 795.
No more than twenty, handcuffed and riding shotgun,
he'd hocked a good one, gleaming oyster tattooing glass.
With three quick cracks the flashlight broke his knee.

I guess he's not the only one you'd hurt, though
you never talked about the others. I'd learned
the lesson that was meant for me: *Don't ever cross
me,* you'd said in other words.

Would it have surprised those boys to see you
here, nose dripping into matted fur? That great
brown body cold and heavy on your lap?
Your shoulders shaking, sobs silent as the sacristy?
Sometimes gentleness confounds a brutal man,
and I can see your bent frame still, leaning on that
kennel while you search for words, some version
of *I'm sorry* no dead dog would hear.

Lion brothers

Sometimes they sent her home early,
her hand bandaged tight where a needle
had pierced her. Home from school,
we found her curled on the floor, watching.

She woke early to put on her face
before we could see it for what it
wasn't, round and smooth and yellow.
Her legs tucked under her,
she held the mirror in her tiny hand
and painted on the jungle colors:
blacks and blues. At the factory
she tied tools around her waist,
slimmer than any boy's, though her arms
were knotted in muscles. She climbed up
beside the men, four feet above the ground
on their vibrating monsters, machines
that worked like animals. Like pieces
of thread cut from the loom and dropped
clean, their words gathered around her feet.

Chink.

It seemed like a child's word
if you didn't know the meaning.

Three on the tree

I was fifteen when he taught me how to turn my palm
toward my face and, with his hand on the back

of mine, we pulled it toward us and dropped it down
into first. The shift into second was the nicest —

our hands resting on the top, arcing toward the sky
until it caught and I could ease out the clutch,

pushing hard on the pedal, a full foot off the floor.
Left one up and right one down until they met

in the middle. It was a tricky, tuneless dance,
but I liked it all the same. Third was our reward,

a hard drop down with no regrets, the truck gently
rocking as we covered mile after hot mile.

He was right about so many things that I've
had some trouble keeping track. Needing

help from time to time, I accept it without
shame. Flat tires and an empty bank account,

sick children and an ego kicked and low,
failures at love and losses beyond any words.

Facing disaster, I think of long spring
days with him beside me, Springsteen belting

words of hope and failure. I place my hands
at 9 and 3 and listen for the engine's roar.

Tiger mother

She stops short of licking them, though
the impulse to nibble on them is strong,
like scent. She will carry them a thousand
miles if she has to, manage them by turns
on her narrow back, find a way to feed
them, digging at the roots with claws bleeding
and black. If need be, she will tear the face
from any living thing with her strong white teeth,
carry them with fangs so gently they will think
they are her own powerful arms grown long
and striped. She will find a place to lay them,
tucked into a depression in the ground she
digs herself and makes soft with leaves.

Maybe this was what her own mother was
thinking when she spoke about those other
things: the length of fingernails, the length
of skirts, the length of hair, the length of time.
Right words. Right work. Right man. Right way.

Instead, she might have said *You are good enough
already. Because I am your mother, I will carry you
on my back, tired as it is, and lay you down
in the darkness to find your own way.*

Trespass

It was Sunday and I was tired, restless
and unsettled in the bone-hard pew.
Just then, I recognized her hair,

that tangled mess of brown she'd had
as a girl, now picked through with gray.
It had been twenty years since I'd seen her last,

but when she turned her face toward me I knew
that blink of blue, that ski-jump nose. Her name was
Ruby. Red, like menstrual blood, the bright

bold knoll of puberty, the knife-blood red of
childhood fresh gone. Gone suddenly,
not the whispered hush of change that happens

slowly, imperceptibly, like forgiveness.

I was fifteen when my father told me what
happened to Ruby and why she moved away.
He told me driving in the car, the way he told me

everything too difficult to face. I thought of Ruby's
father, his cigar-stained hands impatient, folded
over the steering wheel of their old car, while he

waited at the bus stop in the blazing heat.
I thought of days when we'd ignored her on the
playground because she was dirty or we were

tired of pretending that she was our friend.
I wanted to believe we would have been kinder
had we known her father's rough betrayals.

Here in God's house she offered me a sign
of peace, a polite smile bending her lips. Taking
her warm hand in mine, I sought forgiveness for

my trespass, for not knowing what we'd done.
Her face, blank and pale, offered nothing.
She didn't know me from Adam.

Complicity

We wanted to buy them, just
for one day. Three girls and four

boys in khakis and polo shirts.
Girls pooled their money to buy

the cute one whose bangs
nearly covered his eyes.

Preppy auctioneers hawked
their wares with great gusto,

and our slaves, in good spirit,
sported chains made of paper,

colorful rings stuck together
with paste. The room was in riot

when I spotted Miss Miller,
my algebra teacher.

Squeezed into a dress two
sizes too small, trembling,

her hands were clenched
and she was weeping. I asked

my friend, a boy with perfect
teeth, if he knew why. It was

the South in 1985,
and fundraising's changed since then.

The corpse of memory

I believe they still use shock therapy
to snip the strings of memory
in some parts of the world.
Deep in a bunker in North Korea,

for instance, disloyal citizens are
unburdened of their memories
of childhood, of children, of parents, of friends.
The magnolia loses its distinctive taste,

and the hungry belly forgets its grip as
blue tongues of shock lick the brain
in predictable intervals. Gray matter
jiggles loose from its moorings

and frees the mind of those meddlesome
connections, tight tissues that bind
to things that have no value anymore.
If that doesn't work, there is always

lobotomy, performed simply with a straight,
sharp object like, say, a metal nail file
pounded in through the ocular cavity,
so efficient there is hardly any blood.

What if Emerson was wrong when he told
us to drop the corpse of memory?
To leave it, heavy at our feet? When he
urged us to walk away, the dust puffing

upwards as our arms hang slack and newly weightless,
did he think that we'd be free?

Zoonosis

There is no end to the dangers animals pose.
Microscopic deer ticks have the indecency
to leave behind swollen joints, fever

and fatigue after sucking our blood.
Neglected dogs and ordinary raccoons
become bewildered malcontents,

appearing in strange habitats, snapping
at us with their foaming jaws.
And those innocent cows, munching

away in patty-smeared fields, contaminate
our boots and somehow cause our brains to swell.
Instead, what if we passed our crippling

maladies to our animal friends?
When we stroke their backs and scratch
behind their ears, feeling along the tender

depressions in their skulls, what if we infested
them with anxieties, with depression inked in
deepest blue? Suppose we splashed our

traumatic memories in Technicolor across
their innocent brains, paralyzing their senses?
What if, unwittingly, we infected an army

of mosquitoes with our control issues?
Swarming in unison, they would look for ways
to call the shots for every living thing.

Imagine the damage that we'd do.

I had pretty plumage once

The bees alighting on clover so near my toes
have no interest in what I have to offer.
Fat wolf spiders on my porch jump at flies
and leave my arms, my legs, unmolested.
Unnamed snakes that could be copperheads,
but probably aren't, have no business here,
their forked tongues and fisted faces aimed at
other prey. Deer ticks, clinging to a thousand
tall blades, would prefer to jump their perches
for some piece of puppy ass waving
at the sky in happy oblivion; and even
the darkening sky, with its strong, broad
shoulders, seems interested in other things.
Or maybe he doesn't love me anymore.

When I leave you

Don't look for obvious clues,
like the vague scent of alien aftershave
on the blouses I left in our closet.
You'll find no calls to a number you don't
recognize, or piles of oversized clothes
that don't fit me anymore. Good luck
rifling through the trash in search
of crumpled receipts to restaurants
you never frequented. When I leave you,
look for gummy, flesh-colored flakes
swollen fat by water. Those remnants
of your morning oatmeal always
gathering at the bottom of the sink
will tell you why I'm gone.

Cow

Weeks like this one make me wonder how nice
it might be to be a cow just chewing, slowly moving
my jaws in clockwise angles. Frothing green trickles
between my teeth and at the drooping corners of my
single-minded mouth, I could lie down and rest
on legs not asked to move except to escape the winds
and stinging rain that come up from the south sometimes.
Or maybe I'd just stand here, letting the water wash my
tough hide—brown rivers of yesterday's dirt rolling
inevitably down into the holes I'm standing in—
thinking of nothing and no one in particular.

Washing rice

Don't ever ask me where to buy the rice,
or what kind of rice to buy, or how many

times I think you should wash the rice
to remove the starch, or why you should

remove the starch at all. Don't speak to me
in cups of water, in degrees, or in minutes

it should take before the steam appears
and then subsides, showing you the rice

is ready to fork by sticky lumps into your
wide and hungry mouth. Instead, ask me

how the grains feel slipping between each
of my fingers as I draw up handful after

handful from the bottom. Ask me what I
think about when I part the rice from small

streams of water the color of breast milk.
Wonder out loud how swirling it with all

five of my fingers and feeling the sturdy
wholeness of each grain makes me hold

my breath. Make me tell you how trapping
the rice with my hand at the bowl's lip

and tipping it far enough to drain the water
lets me expel my breath, whole and sure

enough to measure the depth of the water
with my hand alone. Ask me how I'll do all

of this for as long as it takes the sun
to set above the trees outside my kitchen

window. Ask me about these things instead,
and I'll tell you nothing you want to hear.

Pre-op

I tried sleeping on my back the whole night, and when
I woke I thought, can I still speak pig Latin?
I made a cup of Earl Grey since the bergamot

makes me sick. I pulled on a sweater the color
of applesauce, the one with sleeves just a little too long.
I squeezed into a pair of scuffed loafers that pinched

my heels in the tenderest places below my smallest toes.
I wore no makeup but painted my nails a bright blue.
Not wanting to give up books, I grabbed the paper

off the counter. I picked the route with six traffic lights,
all timed wrong. I went in through the out door
and hopped into a wheelchair, rolling backwards

beside him. As the nurse took his vitals, I crouched
on the bed, gnawing the sheets. Once he was gone,
I inverted myself against the wall in the waiting room,

head on the floor and heels against the paint, because
people stand upright and I might have to again.

What I learned from William James

This is happiness.

Coffee, strong and black,
is good for me.
The grass will grow slower
now that I've cut it short.
Clothes are clean
and folded and put away.
Humidity is a forgotten dream.
My body expels every toxin
it may have harbored.
(I won't tell you how I know.)
The children favor books
over television. My friends
don't talk about me behind my back.
Flossing means I'll keep my teeth,
and the dog is learning not to tear the carpet.

Happiness is thinking that I'm happy.

Driving home on a cold night after a snowstorm

It's more than quiet, and you realize that's
because the children you always see
playing in the road by that dirty house along
your route are nowhere to be found, their
ugly playthings hidden shallow under
fondant snow. It would be wrong to call it
peaceful, though the snow lies stacked
in neat layers at the base of every wall,
tidying what it can everywhere it touches.
If only you would never see that fat boy
with his mouth wide open, their filthy
dog foraging in the trash, the broken bits
of plastic life piled high by the outbuildings,
those misspelled signs in Day-Glo paint
warning us to keep away. Just then a figure
emerges from the side door, cupping
his hand to protect a flame. Afraid of what
you might see next, you drive a little faster.
In your rearview mirror you see him
standing, more still than the snow, an orange tip
glowing bright like the Christmas lights
someone thought enough to string,
and you think you're almost happy.

In other news

Though Rothko has been dead
for as many years as I've been alive,
I guess I care how he'll take
this latest blow.

In London, a thug with a spray can
defaced a painting in his Seagram series,
one dark gathering of lines
spoiled by another's.

In other news, a mother of five glued
her small child to the wall and beat her senseless,
the grandmother weeping out her testimony
in open court.

Wanting consolation, I look for my husband.
Water spitting into my face over the shower doors,
I shout, *Can you believe someone would do that
to a Rothko?*

Fathers and sons

I wonder if this other Isaac, I mean
the younger boy who lives in my father-in-law's
condo complex in Fort Myers, has any friends?
His father, drunk or stoned in his apartment
all day, has no idea where the son wanders.
Out to the beach to throw shells at birds and waves,
past abandoned towels to gather wallets and shoes,
into the pool where he dives to the bottom
to see how long he can hold his breath
in the water's stinging silence.

The retired veterinarian, tall and tan, befriends him.
They play shuffleboard and pick up trash
along the sidewalk. They put wax on the red
Audi TT and let it dry too long in the sun
before wiping it down. Does the good doctor
sense Isaac's vulnerability?
Is he planning a move when the time is right?
Or maybe, like so many of the warm-blooded
creatures he handled and saved, he'll spare
this stray dog, the one the good mothers
pull their children from. The boy's translucent eyes,
half-hidden behind the fringes of overlong hair,
watch and wait—for what?

Not for the voice of God to save him.

Any dog will bite

Out my kitchen window, I see
my son sitting still on the bank
behind our house. His shoulders
curl forward like a question
mark as he props his elbows
on his knees. The gun,
which looks to me like any real gun,
shoots small plastic pellets
from an orange tip. He stares
unblinking through the sights
arranged on the barrel,
the pink tip of his tongue
exploring his upper lip.
He squeezes the trigger,
nailing the paper target twenty
yards away. Over and over
he reloads and fires, making
tiny adjustments that improve
his aim. I can almost feel
the clicking of good gears
in his eleven-year-old head,
can almost smell the concentration
in his boy's fingers. From here
I can only see the side
of his face, shining with triumph
and maybe something more.
Any dog will bite is one of those
things my father says
from time to time. I know
he means to teach me lessons
until they sink in, like the teeth
of that snapping mongrel he sees
in his head, the dog a stand-in
for everything he fears
or thinks I should.

Gun safe

You said it would make me feel better,
and I guess you're right again. It does.
I am alone, and the house, ordinarily
as quiet as old bones, comes alive.
The dog barks at no one and nothing
in particular as he stares into his reflection
on the paneled windows along the sides
of the front door. And the shadows
that the hall tree casts on the floor
make me feel like there's someone
standing there, even though I know
there isn't. The code to the gun safe
is in my head, burned there by years
of knowing you and the digits of your
birthday: the year, month, and day
your mother pushed you into this
world of private fears and unspoken
desires. My father wore a gun on his
ankle wherever he went, even to church.
I told you it was because of his job,
because he never knew when he'd
have to save a life or take one.
He taught me how to disengage
the safety, how to steady the surprising
weight of any gun in my hands while
I breathe out slowly, pull the trigger,
listen for the explosion, and feel the kick
without blinking. The smell of gun oil
as familiar to me as coffee, I told
you I never wanted one in my home,
that we should live without one
because others said they couldn't.

It's a dangerous gift, knowing just
what others really want. Not the things
they say they want, but what is hidden
in their hearts, buried in the dark, deep
pulse of blood, tucked into the heavy
folds of muscle and complex valves
where no one thinks to look.

Find something else to do
when the holidays come

Go shopping or fly to Aspen or dig yourself a good
deep hole to sit in while you wait for a rain that will
fill it with water until it covers your head
and you can hear your own heart beat again.
(You'll find the quiet a blessing in that cloudy place.)

When you are ready, pull yourself out of the cold water
and into the house so you can drown again between its warm walls,
silent and still as the dust collecting on the banisters.

Don't drive yourself anywhere.

Don't break the hand that's offered to you,
squeezing tightly because you think it might change the outcome.

Don't look for her in someone else's face, seeking her
in the breathing man or woman who takes down your information.

Do listen to the tall, cologned doctor who speaks
with such authority. And whatever you do,

don't look too closely at your girl's face because
she'll look like a stranger, bruised and bloated and still.

When your only child dies on a Wednesday afternoon
playing softball in the bright sun, her lovely
hair spilled into the sand that clings to it,
a gritty corona of gold,
be sure to call your insurance agent (Bob, I think it is)

so he can tell you what to do next.

Mother killer

(in memory of Nancy Lanza)

Last night I dreamed you were a small black bear
come to me from an
unknown place. No one

else recognized it was you, but I would
know the deep set of
your round bright eyes

anywhere, no matter that your bear's eyes
were brown, not blue. You
held me tight with your

thick bear arms, right around the middle where
you used to hold me
when you were small.

You took my hand in your paw to show me
what you'd like to eat,
bright things in crinkly papers,

and I said *No* as gently as I could.
You eat this apple
that I've quartered, or

this peach. After wiping your maw, I said
Let's play nicely with
these boys and girls. No

kicking or biting, bear. Be nice. Next I
showed you how to write
your name in big

broad letters, and you wrote them clearly
so the others could

read them without my

help. We did these things again and again
until you grew tired
and rubbed your eyes. I

put you to bed, stroking your ear until
you closed your eyes and
your mouth fell open,

exposing crooked rows of sharp white teeth.
They told me I was
crazy, whispered lies

about my little bear. *He will not hurt
anyone,* I said,
almost believing

it myself. Studying your long thick claws,
I thought maybe I'd
just chew them down while

you slept, little bear, just as I did when
you were a baby
and had fingernails

like paper. When I closed my eyes too long,
our dream was over.
I missed you, wanted

you close enough to wrap my human arms
and legs around
your wild limbs so tight

you would settle into this stillness
that would have been your whole
world had you let it.

Maybe next time

There's nothing wrong here,
the way they go about their days
while I tap at keys or retreat to my bed.

Racing to the woods to hunt
for speckled salamanders and spade-
foot toads, they'll bob in and out of shredded

light, flanked by stout oaks
and paper birches, sycamores and pine.
They'll spot pink crayfish in silver streams

and look for fox babies
hidden under cool outcroppings
blanketed with lichen. Jumping from rock

to far rock, scaling sharp cliffs
with tight grips and hand boosts, they
are prey to deer ticks, poison ivy, and mosquitoes.

Molested by thorns, skin slippery
with humidity, they will carry in their small
hands long, sharp sticks to protect them, waving them

like swords and poking at the world
unfamiliar before today. When they come home,
they will find me standing at the window sipping my

second glass of Tanqueray, which always tastes to me
like pine cones.

Acknowledgments

Grateful acknowledgment is made to the editors of the following publications who published versions of these poems, sometimes under different titles:

Barrow Street: "In other news"
Bateau: "They say Alfred Hitchcock was afraid of lawmen"
The Delaware Poetry Review: "Cow," "Pre-op," "Trespass"
Frontiers: A Journal of Women Studies: "Lion brothers"
Memoir Journal: "Three on the tree"
Naugatuck River Review: "Fathers and sons"
Orange Coast Review: "The corpse of memory," "Find something else to do when the holidays come"
Potomac Review: "Zoonosis," "Any dog will bite"
Slippery Elm: "Mother killer"
Slipstream: "I had pretty plumage once"
Tar River Poetry: "Driving home on a cold night after a snow storm"

"White" was chosen by Naomi Shihab Nye as the winner of the 2012 *Split This Rock* Poetry Contest.

Thanks to Grant Disharoon and Tom Bligh for their ceaseless support of the work.

Cover artwork and design, "Lament," by Elizabeth Holtry; author photo by Ken Bruggeman; interior book design by Diane Kistner; Cochin text and titling

About FutureCycle Press

FutureCycle Press is dedicated to publishing lasting English-language poetry books, chapbooks, and anthologies in both print-on-demand and ebook formats. Founded in 2007 by long-time independent editor/publishers and partners Diane Kistner and Robert S. King, the press incorporated as a nonprofit in 2012. A number of our editors are distinguished poets and writers in their own right, and we have been actively involved in the small press movement going back to the early seventies.

The FutureCycle Poetry Book Prize and honorarium is awarded annually for the best full-length volume of poetry we publish in a calendar year. Introduced in 2013, our Good Works projects are anthologies devoted to issues of universal significance, with all proceeds donated to a related worthy cause. Our Selected Poems series highlights contemporary poets with a substantial body of work to their credit; with this series we strive to resurrect work that has had limited distribution and is now out of print.

We are dedicated to giving all of the authors we publish the care their work deserves, making our catalog of titles the most diverse and distinguished it can be, and paying forward any earnings to fund more great books.

We've learned a few things about independent publishing over the years. We've also evolved a unique, resilient publishing model that allows us to focus mainly on vetting and preserving for posterity the most books of exceptional quality without becoming overwhelmed with bookkeeping and mailing, fundraising activities, or taxing editorial and production "bubbles." To find out more about what we are doing, come see us at www.futurecycle.org.

www.ingramcontent.com/pod-product-compliance
Lightning Source LLC
Chambersburg PA
CBHW061200040426
42445CB00013B/1763